Winning Ways

for Early Childhood Professionals

Becoming a Team Player

Gigi Schweikert

Name: ______________________________

Date: ______________________________

Redleaf Press®
www.redleafpress.org
800-423-8309

Also in the Winning Ways series from Redleaf Press

Supporting Positive Behavior
Responding to Behavior
Guiding Challenging Behavior
Being a Professional
Partnering with Families
Understanding Infants
Understanding Toddlers and Twos
Understanding Preschoolers
Being a Supervisor

Published by Redleaf Press
10 Yorkton Court
St. Paul, MN 55117
www.redleafpress.org

First edition 2012
Cover design by Jim Handrigan
Cover photograph © Blend Images Photography / Veer
Interior design by Erin Kirk New
Printed in the United States of America

Library of Congress Cataloging-in-Publication Data
Schweikert, Gigi, 1962–
Winning ways for early childhood professionals : becoming a team player / Gigi Schweikert. — 1st ed.
p. cm.
ISBN 978-1-60554-003-0 (alk. paper)
1. Early childhood teachers—United States. 2. Early childhood educators—United States. I. Title.
LB1775.6.S39 2012
372.1100973—dc23
2011026614

Printed on acid-free paper U15-06

Contents

From the Desk of Gigi Schweikert

This is me presenting.

Dear Winning Ways Reader (and Team Player),

When I was young, I used to play teacher. I set up a make-believe classroom with learning centers and activities and then carefully placed my stuffed animals and dolls around to represent the children in my class. Looking back, I never made my teddy bear the coteacher, my doll the assistant teacher, or my Barbie the director. The only teacher was me. I did anything I wanted and ran the classroom the way I liked. I'm still a little like that—I like to do things my way. Can you relate?

Upon entering a real early childhood classroom, I quickly learned that working with other adults is as much a part of the job as working with children, and my way isn't the only way. Learning to work together as a team was difficult for me and it still is. But now I realize that I can't care for and educate a group of children all by myself.

I think you'll really enjoy this Winning Ways book about becoming a team player. We're in this field for the children, and children benefit from having many adults who love and care for them. So these days, I'm more patient with other adults and hope they'll be that way with me. I try to see the perspective of others and think, "How would I want to be treated?"

After you've read *Becoming a Team Player*, share your thoughts with me about creating a great team. We can all use more ideas on how to get along better with others. E-mail me at www.gigischweikert.com.

Children deserve our winning ways,

Introduction

Are You a Team Player?

Are you a team player at work? Most people think they are, yet many people really aren't team players at all. So what is a team player? A team player in early childhood education is someone who puts the needs of the children and their families before anything else. Team players believe that the care and education of children and their families is the primary goal of the profession, and they will do whatever it takes to make those interactions and experiences positive and meaningful. Team players are focused on working hard even when others aren't. Team players don't just point out problems or areas that need improvement—they fix them. Team players follow the rules, help other adults succeed, and genuinely love their jobs, never expecting recognition or praise.

Team players are all about doing their jobs well despite the attitudes of others, overcoming barriers—even when it's easier to complain—and thinking about the needs of others before their own. Sound like a tough job? You bet. That's why most of us aren't team players all the time, and that includes me. Putting others first in a *me first* society is not an easy task for anyone, but it's an essential attribute when working with young children, because they depend on you.

What Makes a Team Player?

Many factors determine a team player in any field. Good team players

- Work together toward a common goal
- Understand that although different jobs have different responsibilities and accountabilities, all positions on a team are equally important

- Are open to innovation and change
- Recognize that there is usually more than one right way to do things
- Discuss concerns and issues
- Share successes and accomplishments
- Constantly think about, reflect on, and discuss aspects of the team
- Help complete less desirable tasks
- Give and receive help during difficult times
- Expect that there will be periodic tension and conflict to work through
- Communicate openly and directly
- Trust and respect each other and the work everyone is doing
- Take care of themselves

The diversity of early childhood professionals on any team creates a rich environment of care and education. Nonetheless, team members must agree upon and follow certain basic principles and practices. Being a team player means that you must communicate frequently with others and be the best that you can be. When you really care about children, you care about how your team functions, because it takes a team to care for children. If you, as a team player, take responsibility for your actions and professionalism, your team improves. Isn't that what everyone wants?

winning ways

A group of kindergarten children went on a field trip to NASA to see the space shuttle. On the trip, the children met many different people. "What do you do?" the children asked the engineer. "I help people to go to the moon. I build the spaceships." Upon seeing an astronaut, the children asked the same question: "What do you do?" The astronaut replied, "I help people go to the moon. I drive the spaceship." At the end of the day, the children saw a gentleman who was sweeping the floor. Again the children asked, "What do you do?" The janitor replied with pride, "I help people go to the moon." The children seemed puzzled, and one asked, "But how do you help people go to the moon by sweeping the floor?" The man smiled at the child and said, "Everyone in this building helps people go to the moon. We all do different jobs, but each job is just as important as the others. We need everyone on our team to do a job, or no one could go to the moon."

Using This Book

Becoming a Team Player consists of ten simple yet powerful steps to help you assess your current attitude as a team player and learn ways to improve your interactions with other team members. Whether tomorrow is your first day on the job or you've been teaching for twenty years, everyone can use a little help when it comes to working more effectively with other adults. If you work at an early childhood program full-time, you spend more time with the people at work than you do with members of your own family. Don't children deserve to be surrounded by adults who are committed to making their team, or work family, as strong and functional and loving as it can be? Of course. Check out the sections below and look for ways that you and the others in your program can be a winning team.

1 Be Respectful and Professional
2 Encourage Others
3 Appreciate the Lives of Others
4 Take Care of Yourself
5 Don't Gossip
6 Share Your Talents
7 Be a Problem Solver
8 Arrive on Time
9 Get Organized and Return Things You Borrow
10 Don't Judge Others

How a Team Functions

Different team positions come with different responsibilities and accountability, but all the positions on your team are equally important. Working well with other adults positively affects the quality of care and education of the children.

Good teamwork starts with your conscious decision to do your best regardless of how others perform.

Stay Positive!

Here are a few things to avoid:

- Trying to change other adults
- Thinking one job is more important than another
- Believing that if other adults would just do things the way you want, your team would improve

Make It Happen! Here's How

Who's important on your team? The janitor in the NASA story understands the importance of a well-functioning team and how it really works. He realizes that every person in an organization is equally important to accomplishing the goal of the program. Does sweeping the floor at NASA really help to get a person on the moon? You bet. You can't work in a building that's not clean and safe.

Think about the people who work in your program: the teachers, the director, the building-maintenance professionals. Does each job carry different responsibilities and accountability? Sure, but each job is equally important to providing good care and education for children. If there's a position in a program that doesn't contribute to helping educate and care for children, it's probably not needed. So who's important in a team? Everyone is, and that includes you.

Do You Work Well with Other Adults?

Most people go into early childhood education because they like working with children. Working with children is your passion. It's what you do well. It's the adults that can be a bit challenging at times. Nonetheless, working well with adults is just as important as the work you do with children in this field.

Why is it important for a team of adults to function well? A great team is vital to any company, but in early childhood education, the compatibility of the adults doesn't just affect getting the job done; it also affects the emotional and social environment of children.

Why Is Good Teamwork so Important in Early Childhood Education?

Think of it like this: in your environment, the team of adults you work with and the children you serve are like a family. Children look to you for their physical and emotional safety. They may not know that at home their parents aren't getting along, but they can sense discord in their environments. The same is true for their early childhood team: when the adults aren't working well as a team, the care and education of the children is not as excellent as it could be. Children can sense the tension and that's not good for them or you.

Being a good team doesn't mean that there won't be disagreements at times or different points of view. It's normal and good for centers and schools to continually question and discuss how the program should run. What's important is how you share your differences, resolve the issues, and represent your team despite your different perspectives.

Just as children can sense dissonance among adults, they can also sense harmony. When you are laughing with your coteachers in the presence of the children, having a good time and communicating well, the children benefit from the positive environment, and you accomplish the work. How you conduct yourself and interact with others on your team is one of the most effective teaching tools you have. It is much more effective than gluing cotton balls onto a sheet of construction paper. You try to teach children lots of lessons, and what is more fundamental than role-modeling how to get along with others?

This Team Would Be Great If Everyone Else Would Just . . .

Are you thinking, "I'm willing to work with other adults, but sometimes they aren't willing to work with me. If other people would just change!" Do you ever wish others would

- Do things without being asked
- Do what you ask
- Do things the way you do them
- Change

At times, all of us wish that other people would change how they carry out their job responsibilities. Some people probably think that about you too. Ouch! Yes, many of us are set on changing other people. But here's what I know: you can change diapers, but you can't change people.

One of the interesting things about the concept of teamwork is that people typically think that if everybody else would do what they were suppose to do, they'd have a good team. "If she would just put the glue back."

"If he would just return the stuff he borrowed." "If she would just have a better attitude. "If he would just show up on time." "If she wouldn't gossip." Do you think these kinds of things about other people? Yes, absolutely—we all do. Well, here's the scoop: the most important tip you're ever going to get about a winning team is that teamwork starts with you. Teamwork is not about how we change other people. We can guide adults, coach adults, lead adults, motivate adults, and affirm adults. That's all good stuff that can help a team. In desperation, we can even try to shame, humiliate, or alienate adults to try to get them to do what we want them to do. That's wrong, and it doesn't help the team or anyone else. Either way, adults, just like children, are ultimately going to make their own choices.

How Do You Improve Your Team If Changing Others Isn't the Answer?

You can't change other people. You can only change yourself and how you react to others. A winning team starts with you. If you can't change others, how do you improve your team? You can make your team stronger by being the best person you can be and by being a role model for others. It's your responsibility as a member of your team to coach, assist, and support other adults to become the best team players they can be. Other people will never be like you, so stop wishing that. Other adults can become something even better: they can become the best persons and team players they can be.

How Can You Be a Better Team Player?

There's room for improvement in us all. Start with a self-assessment, then move on to the ten steps that will help you become a better team player. You might not have heard of some of the steps. If that's the case, I hope they will enlighten and encourage you to become a better team member. Many of the steps you may know and have forgotten or just aren't practicing. In any situation, I hope you will open your mind to honestly assess how you interact with other adults and what steps you can take to improve those interactions regardless of how other team members behave. Remember this: teamwork is about what you can do for the other adults you work with, not about what they can do for you.

SELF-ASSESSMENT

Why Don't Adults Always Do Their Best?

If everyone focuses on doing their best, will you have a good team? That's the premise. And here's the challenge: people don't always do their best. Sometimes they don't give their best because they don't know how. They need the education, coaching, and encouragement of others on the team. Sometimes adults don't do their best because they aren't motivated or just don't want to work. That's a performance issue that their supervisor needs to address. But most people aren't the best team players they can be because they haven't accurately assessed themselves. They don't realize they could be performing better. Too much time is spent worrying about how others act or should act, instead of focusing on their own behavior.

Why Adults Don't Always Perform Well

Reason	How to Help
"I don't know how." Lack of knowledge.	Offer education, workshops, and resources.
"I can't do it well." Lack of experience.	Provide role-modeling, coaching, and opportunities to practice.
"I'm scared I'll mess up." Fear of failure.	Offer encouragement and support. Reduce the risks of failure.
"I don't want to." Lack of motivation.	Ask their reasons for not doing their work. Provide support as well as consequences for lack of performance.

Assessing Yourself

Before you begin the following self-assessment, take a few minutes to read the directions.

Directions for self-assessment. Read each of the ten statements below and then assign yourself a number 1 through 5. A 1 means you are extremely accomplished in this attribute, and a 5 indicates that you rarely exhibit this characteristic.

Some of these things may be done some of the time, but to create a really supportive work environment, these things need to be done all of the time. Because you spend so much of your time with your team members, make your work family terrific!

1 I speak with other adults in a respectful and professional manner.

Always Usually Sometimes Never

2 I encourage, support, and nurture other adults.

Always Usually Sometimes Never

3 I take time to understand and appreciate the lives, values, and personal priorities of other adults.

Always Usually Sometimes Never

4 During work, I take time for myself to focus my thoughts and to renew my physical strength and mental outlook.

Always Usually Sometimes Never

5 I do not participate in gossip, and I speak directly to other adults with whom I have questions or issues.

Always Usually Sometimes Never

6 I share my own special skills and expertise with other adults.

Always Usually Sometimes Never

7 Without being asked, I help others by proposing and carrying out creative solutions and improving problematic situations.

Always Usually Sometimes Never

8 I am prepared for work by being on time.

Always Usually Sometimes Never

9 I organize my workspace and share my resources with other adults. I respect the workspace of other adults by asking before I borrow something and returning it when I am finished.

Always Usually Sometimes Never

10 I talk with other adults in real conversations about what there are doing and thinking and do not judge but try to understand.

Always Usually Sometimes Never

Using Your Self-Assessment

There are a few teachable moments about teamwork in the preceding self-assessment. First, how many of you started or completed the self-assessment without reading the directions? The form looked pretty simple, right? Ten statements with four adverbs describing the frequency of each step. Who needs directions? Right?

Did You Skip the Directions?

It's worth noting why you may have completed the assessment without reading the directions. You're a doer. You want to get things done. You see things that need doing, and you want to complete them. Sound like you? Did you skip the directions? That's okay, and probably that's what I would have done—but keep in mind that when team members don't take the time to follow directions or read correspondence, they often miss things. Whether you're an experienced teacher or new to the field, take the time to read and listen to directions. Even if you think you know how to do something or have done it a hundred times, there's always something new to learn.

Were You Confused by the Directions?

If you read the directions, were they confusing? You bet! I asked you to use numbers to rate yourself, and the form has words that imply you circle or mark them in some way. You may have disregarded my directions and circled answers anyway. Or you may have tried to follow the directions but were uncomfortable because they didn't make sense. Or you may have done both: rated yourself using the numbers and circled the frequency words. What did you do?

Teamwork Requires Good Communication and Directions

There's another teachable moment here. The written directions said one thing and the layout of the form implied another. Teamwork requires communicating effectively and asking questions when you don't understand. The directions you read and the visual implications of the form were different, confusing, and they set you up to fail.

People often get frustrated by the actions or inactions of others. Do you help people succeed by communicating well? Or do you assume other team members will see what needs to be done and do it as you want?

Good Communication for Those Giving the Directions

Often others can't do what is requested of them because they just don't understand what is wanted. When other adults aren't performing well or being good team players, you have to ask yourself these questions:

- Was my communication effective, or did I set up people to fail?
- Did I communicate at all or just assume the person would know what to do and how to do it?
- Did I communicate in a variety of ways?
- Did I give people a chance to ask questions to ensure they understood?

Good Communication for Those Receiving the Directions

Keep in mind that a winning team begins with you. Not understanding what you are supposed to do for the team isn't an excuse for not performing. You can't use old excuses like "Well, I didn't know," or "No one told me." When you are working on a team, especially one that cares for children, you must take responsibility for doing things right, even if others get it wrong.

- Don't use excuses for inaction or incorrect action.
- Act when you see that something needs to be done, even if no one asks you.
- Ask questions if you don't understand.
- Don't gauge how much work you should do by comparing yourself to others around you. Do your best regardless of their actions.

Good Communication for Us All

So whether you are giving or receiving directions, being a team player means taking responsibility and doing your best. What should be done to succeed and create a stronger team?

- Read all communication thoroughly.
- Ask questions if you don't understand.
- Follow the directions you are given.

Bonus Question

Did you see the typo in the self-assessment form?

What did seeing a mistake in a published book make you think? Not very professional, right? The first step to creating a winning team is being respectful and professional. As educators, correct spelling and grammar in our written communication are important. They convey our professionalism and advance and maintain our credibility. Have others read over your work before you hand it out.

Where was the typo? In question 10, I wrote *there* when the word should have been *they.* Did you catch it?

10 Steps to a Winning Team

Even if you circled "Always," be sure to read the corresponding step: there's always something to learn and improve on. Refer back to your completed self-assessment form as you explore the ten steps to creating a winning team. Let's get going to create a winning team!

STEP 1

Be Respectful and Professional

1

I speak with other adults in a respectful and professional manner.

- Always
- Usually
- Sometimes
- Never

Are You Really Respectful and Professional?

Do you feel you are usually respectful and professional? Most of us would probably rate ourselves as "Usually" being respectful and professional and some of us "Always." Perhaps that's a true assessment, but I want you to really think about your interactions with other adults.

The early childhood field is typically full of professionals who are nurturing, kind, and patient by nature. Hey, you care for children, and usually people who are easily frustrated, impatient, and grumpy don't go into this field, at least not for long. Those positive qualities are a good thing when it comes to working with adults as well. You don't usually yell at others on your team or raise your voice when you are frustrated or upset. It's unlikely that you would go over to another adult and scream, "What the matter with you? Why didn't you put the top back on the glue?" That would be really unprofessional, and for most of us, it's just not in our nature.

How Do You Act at Work When You Are Upset?

So what do you do when you are frustrated or upset? Sometimes it looks like this. You are upset with another staff member, but you don't tell her why. You feel frustrated, but you don't say anything to her. You arrive for your shift and enter the classroom. She enthusiastically asks, "How are you doing this morning?" You reply flatly, "Fine." She makes another attempt to speak nicely to you and says, "It's so gorgeous outside. We could take the kids to the park this morning and maybe have snack outside. Would you like to do that?" Without looking at her, you respond in a barely audible monotone, "Whatever you want." So she tries once again to get you to speak up, to converse: "Is everything okay?" Once again, you utter quietly, "Yes, everything is fine."

What's happening? You are not telling her what's on your mind. And you're giving her the cold shoulder. You may not even realize it, or your behavior may be very intentional. Are your answers to her questions disrespectful and unprofessional in content or tone? Somewhat. Are they productive to the team? Not at all! You are upset with her, but she doesn't know why, and she can't correct the problem if she doesn't know what it is. Your behavior really isn't respectful or professional—and what's worse, the children can often sense such tension.

Disrespectful and Unprofessional Behavior: Are You Guilty?

There are many ways for early childhood professionals to be disrespectful to others besides giving someone the cold shoulder or yelling, accusing, or threatening. Some of these other tactics can be just as hurtful. Take a look at the following list. Are you guilty? Do you

1. Pretend everything is fine when you are upset
2. Convey your frustration through subtle but inappropriate facial expressions
3. Exaggerate your movements in the room by walking loudly, closing cabinets forcefully, or placing things down with great effort
4. Refuse to talk with someone or say only what is absolutely necessary
5. Talk to someone in a slightly frustrated tone
6. Deny that you are upset even when another adult asks you directly
7. Avoid the person with whom you are upset
8. Let things that upset you go when they really matter to you

Do You Avoid Issues That Are Bothering You?

When people are upset, they often respond by avoiding the situation or the other person involved. When a person doesn't like confrontation, instead of telling someone exactly what she thinks, she just decides, "I'm not going to say anything." She convinces herself that it's not a big deal and decides to put a big smile on her face and be the best person she can be. Isn't that a good way to behave, since creating a winning team starts with each person being the best she can be? Not in this case, because the person is not being the best person she can be. She has an issue, and instead of discussing it respectfully and professionally with the other staff member, she decides not to say anything at all.

What happens over time when someone continually avoids the issue? All of the things that have been avoided are eventually brought to the surface by a seemingly innocuous action. Take a look. All of a sudden, you or one of your coworkers is absolutely upset and frustrated because someone didn't put the puppets back where they were supposed to go. But it wasn't the puppets that were the problem. The puppets being out of place was merely the domino that caused all the other issues to tip. It's the simple domino effect of things building up for months or even years because the team didn't know how you felt and what you thought.

Think Before You Speak

Now, I am not suggesting that tomorrow you approach your team and share all the things that have been bothering you over the past several years. Resist the urge to spout something like "I want to tell you something. Let me start with the fact that I don't like those jeans, and you've had them for ten years, and then let me tell you that when you do circle time, you're boring. And then let me tell you that you never return the things you borrow, and on top of that, your art projects are messy." That's not what I'm implying at all. That type of tirade is certainly not respectful and professional. It's critical, rude, and hurtful. It won't help create a better team—that type of personal attack will destroy a team.

Here's my suggestion: if you want a winning team, when issues arise that are significant to the care of children, then you need to discuss them. Tell the person with whom you have an issue what's on your mind.

Does It Really Matter?

How are you going to know if something is significant enough to discuss or not? Here's how you are going to know. You're going to ask yourself, "Does it really matter?" Imagine that you are upset about the way the front lobby looks. You've told people to keep it neat, and it's messy, and that makes you upset. Ask yourself before you start to give people the cold shoulder, avoid the issue, stuff your frustrations away, or freak out on all the people who are responsible for that lobby area, "Does it really matter?" And here's how you know if it really matters: you ask yourself a second question, "How does it affect the children?"

By asking yourself "Does it really matter?" and "How does it affect the children?" you begin to assess if your frustration is a result of your over-controlling, perfectionist, crazy, uptight personality, which demands that the lobby look a certain way, or if the messy lobby really affects the children in a negative way. Think about it. It affects the children in a negative way if they are going to trip and get hurt. It affects the children in a negative way if parents walk in and think, "I'm paying what for this, and everything is a mess." When parents are upset and angry, their children may sense these emotions. The parent's angry feelings about the messy lobby may go straight from that parent to their child, and then everyone becomes uptight. All from a messy lobby? You bet. So does a messy and unsafe lobby affect the children? Absolutely.

You need to differentiate between your own feelings of control and *doing it your way* and *how it affects the children.* If something affects the children in a negative way, then you are under obligation to say something to the person responsible or go to your supervisor if you need help and support to talk with another coworker—no cold shoulder or avoidance allowed. Is it easy to do? No. But is it the respectful and professional thing to do? Absolutely.

12 Ways to Treat Others Respectfully and Professionally

1. Greet people enthusiastically.
2. Smile even when you don't feel like it.
3. Use your manners. Say, "Please," "Thank you," and "Excuse me."
4. Ask questions if you don't understand what someone is saying or doing.
5. Speak up about issues that directly or indirectly affect the care and education of the children.
6. Listen more than you speak.
7. Ask others how they feel.
8. Give people the benefit of the doubt.
9. Don't let little things get to you.
10. Enjoy your job.
11. Have a sense of humor.
12. Realize that a winning team starts with you.

winning ways

Did you assess yourself as "Always" for this first step about being respectful and professional? It is easy to think that you are respectful and professional all the time until you start to look at the more subtle ways an early childhood educator can be disrespectful or unprofessional. Behaviors such as not smiling, avoiding talking with another adult with whom you have an issue, or just letting things go are unprofessional. So how would you assess yourself on this question now? Being respectful and professional is a lot more complicated than you think. The next step is encouraging others. Nurturing children may be your strong point, but how are you at nurturing and encouraging adults?

OPTIMIZE YOUR KNOWLEDGE

1 List three ways in which a professional in any field can behave **disrespectfully** or **unprofessionally.**

1 ______________________________

2 ______________________________

3 ______________________________

2 Explain your own tendencies in exhibiting disrespectful or unprofessional behavior. What can you do to **change** those tendencies?

____

____

____

____

____

____

3 Survey two other early childhood professionals and list what they believe are three ways to show **professionalism** and **respect.** Are their lists similar to or different from yours and each other?

1 ______________________________

2 ______________________________

3 ______________________________

1 ______________________________

2 ______________________________

3 ______________________________

STEP 2

Encourage Others

2

I encourage, support, and nurture other adults.

- Always
- Usually
- Sometimes
- Never

Do You Encourage Other Adults?

If the statement read "I encourage, support, and nurture *children*," you would definitely have answered, "Always," right? That's what you do best: nurture and encourage children. How about adults? How did you rate your encouragement quotient with regard to adults? (*Sometimes? Usually? Never?*) Adults, like children, need lots of encouragement, and that's what good team members give each other. People on a winning team encourage each other to be the best they can be. The strength of any team is only as strong as the weakest member, and everyone needs a little encouragement sometimes.

Did you know that even geese at the back of a formation honk to encourage those up front to maintain their speed? This type of honking, or encouragement, inspires the lead geese to do their best, to know that they are part of a group. We're not talking here about the annoying honking that people tend to do on traffic-jammed highways where honking is not going to get anyone moving.

How Can You Encourage Other Adults?

Find a blank piece of paper and something to write with. Think about an adult with whom you work and something she has done recently that's worth noting. Now write that person a note of encouragement to tell her what a good job she did or how much you appreciate her. One last direction before you get started: you only have one minute to write the note. On your mark, get set, go!

How long did it take you to write the note? Only a minute or less. That's a lot of encouragement in a short amount of time, a good return on your investment. So what does the person who receives the note do? Does she read it, crumble it up, and toss it away? Hardly. When you receive an encouraging note from someone, you read it again and again. You send it to your mother, read it to your husband, and show it to your kids. Oh, yeah! It makes you feel good! That's what you do every day for kids. Think of the encouraging things you say to children: Good job! Way to go! You can do it! Come on! But this isn't always done for adults. Somehow you think, "They're all grown-ups. How much support and nurturing do they really need?" But adults need, you need, everyone needs as much encouragement as children do each and every day. Encourage the adults on your team as much as you do the children in your classroom.

How Do You Encourage Adults Who Are Struggling?

Now do that exercise once more, this time with a twist. Think of an adult you work with who is struggling a bit, dealing with a demanding parent, trying to help a challenging child, or working to stay within a tight budget. Notes of encouragement don't need to be sent just for a job well done. Notes of encouragement can also acknowledge the efforts of people who are working hard to find a solution to overcome a problem, to do a better job. You have sixty seconds—what would you write? Here are a couple of notes that teachers have written for others members of their teams.

Dear Teammate,

You are working so hard to help the child in your room use his words instead of hitting. Situations like that can be exhausting. What a gift that child has with you on his side.

Sincerely,
Your Teammate

Dear Teammate,

I know that it can be difficult when children transition up to a new class. You'll soon feel the same love for your new group of children as you did for the last.

Sincerely,
Your Teammate

Keep Encouraging the Members of Your Team

Don't wait for members of your team to ask for help. If someone realizes that you are willing to give your time and energy to help her, she is less likely to give up on herself. If this really is a team, isn't another person's struggle really your struggle too?

30 Things You Can Say to Encourage an Adult

1 I'm so glad we work together.
2 You have so many good ideas.
3 Thanks for helping.
4 You always share everything in your room. We should all be more like you.
5 You've really been patient in this situation.
6 Just try again. Sometimes it takes a couple of tries to get it right.
7 I've learned so much from you.
8 You make it fun to work here.
9 I know you can do it.
10 Let me know if you need some help.
11 Are you having a difficult time?
12 Don't worry.
13 Great job.
14 You're really determined to make it work.
15 Tell me how you feel.
16 Well done.
17 Don't give up!
18 It's okay to make a mistake.
19 You're really working hard, and I notice that.
20 That was a really creative activity you planned.
21 You're a good listener.
22 I appreciate your contributions.
23 It's hard when things don't go as we planned.
24 This program just wouldn't be the same without you.
25 I'm so glad you work here.
26 What a dedicated professional you are.
27 Your sense of humor keeps me going.
28 Thanks for telling me how you feel. It's not always easy to say what's on your mind.
29 You're always willing to lend an extra hand.
30 Keep going.

When you initially think about working with young children, you don't often think about working with adults, especially not about nurturing and encouraging them. Yet all of us in early childhood education, or any profession, can always benefit from a kind word. It feels good when others notice and acknowledge our good work, and it feels even better if others help when we are struggling. The third team-building step is Appreciate the Lives of Others.

OPTIMIZE YOUR KNOWLEDGE

1 Give yourself sixty seconds to write **a short note of encouragement** to a coworker or another adult. Draft it here, then give the person the note on a clean piece of paper.

2 Using the list **30 Things You Can Say to Encourage an Adult**, check the things you have done personally to encourage others. Then circle three ways that you will try to encourage others in the future.

3 Name a **struggle** you have experienced working in early childhood education or in your life and assess how others have helped you. List additional ways you could have been helped.

STEP 3

Appreciate the Lives of Others

3

I take time to understand and appreciate the lives, values, and personal priorities of other adults

- Always
- Usually
- Sometimes
- Never

Is It Possible to Leave Your Life at the Workplace Door?

You may have been told many times that you should leave your life at the door, but is that really possible? To a certain extent it has to be. Because you work with children, you can't allow your personal life interfere with competently caring for the children. Everyone can agree that children are the first priority. To create a winning team, you have to find a way to help *all* team members balance their work, life responsibilities, and priorities. And that's hard to do.

So let's take a look at your answer to step 3, "I take time to understand and appreciate the lives, values and personal priorities of other adults." I'm not sure any of us can answer "Always" to that statement, given that most of us have busy lives ourselves. And the sad thing in many teams is that you may have worked with others for a number of years and really do not know much about their lives at all. Is it necessary to know the personal lives of others to create a great team? No, you don't need to know every detail, and some people prefer to keep their private lives private. That's okay, too, but as a team member, you must help others, and sometimes that includes helping them cope with personal issues.

Help Others Balance Work and Life Issues

To sustain itself over time, a winning team needs to understand and appreciate the personal priorities of its members. Here's another goose example.

> When a goose becomes sick, wounded, or shot down, two geese drop out of formation and follow it down to help and protect it. They stay with it until it dies or is able to fly again. Then they launch out with another formation or catch up with the flock. (Robert McNeish, "Lessons from the Geese," 1972)

That's compassion and empathy and putting others first. That's teamwork. Can you help the members of your team by rallying around them, supporting them, and helping them until they can rejoin their formation?

Why should you help others in this way when their personal lives aren't part of the job? Well, for one, you are a nurturing and caring person. It's the right thing to do. Beyond that, everyone can achieve more as a team than individually. Each team member needs to be at his or her best. I think that is forgotten sometimes. You are more productive as a team, whether supporting someone in a time of need or running a program, than you are as an individual. No matter how amazing you are, you don't have enough energy or coffee to do it on your own. It takes a whole team to run a program.

What's Happening in the Lives of the People You Work With?

People experience certain things in their lives that require us to rally around them. Day-to-day issues may include a broken car, sickness, an argument with a spouse, or home problems, such as flooding. More devastating issues include illness, death of a loved one, divorce, money problems, or substance abuse.

Dealing with Daily Issues

How do you deal with such day-to-day issues? Good communication. "My car broke down; I'm going to be late." "I feel a bit tired today. I just wanted you to know that in case I don't seem as energetic as usual." By communicating what is happening in your life to those on your team, you allow other members to support you and pick up the slack until you can get back into formation. You'll do the same for them when they have daily distractions.

Dealing with More Devastating Issues in Life

How do you help team members with the big issues in life? It's one thing to occasionally cover for someone whose car breaks down, but what do you do about the really big things such as illness and alcoholism? First and most important, you need to make sure staff members get the professional help they need. You cannot take the place of doctors, counselors, or other professionals. Here are some things you—with your supervisors and the Human Resource departments—can do:

- Realize that with the exception of the director, you don't need to know the details of anyone's personal issues unless she chooses to tell you. You have to trust your administrators to deal with that part.
- Listen and ask how you can help if a person chooses to share specifics with you. Keep in mind that many times a person just wants someone to talk to, not necessarily someone who will solve her problems.
- Keep these conversations from children unless it affects them or it is necessary that they know—for example, when someone is losing hair as a result of chemo. In such a situation, look to the administrators to guide you on what is developmentally appropriate to share with children.
- Maintain the person's confidentiality. Some people like to share their personal concerns and others are very private. Respect their choices.
- Understand that many people want to work when problems arise in their lives. Many need the financial compensation, and most appreciate the diversion and normalcy that working provides during a chaotic time.
- Let the administrators, other professionals, and the team member herself decide if she is capable of continuing to work directly with children during this time.

How Do You Help the Person Who Always Has Problems?

Unfortunately, some people experience a series of tragedies in their lives, and their resulting, inconsistent work patterns may affect the care of the children. That's doesn't mean you don't work to help them. In these extreme cases, the administrators must balance assisting the employee with maintaining continuity and quality of care for the children.

Helping the Complaining Team Member

Some people always seem to have problems and to generally complain or be negative. Initially, you must try to help these team members too. They may be employees who are often late because of a missed bus or who are frequently tired and can't perform their job responsibilities to expectation. Can you help them brainstorm some transportation solutions or ask questions to understand why they say negative things about the program? Just as you work tirelessly to help every child succeed, you need to do the same for adults. Exhaust every resource and opportunity you have to help people who constantly have problems to overcome them and succeed. If the team's tireless efforts are not helping this employee become a more positive team player, the administrators may need to step in. Not all people work well in early childhood education. Perhaps their skills are better suited for another field.

Sometimes It Doesn't Seem Fair That One Team Member Is Getting All the Attention

Sometimes it does feel as if one team member is monopolizing much of the program's efforts, but if that person were you, wouldn't you want the help too? Fair is not always equal. Think about caring for children: you make sure that each one gets individual care and attention, but on certain days some children get more attention than others. A child falls down and gets hurt. A child is very fussy. A child is new to the program. You work hard to make sure each one receives the love and nurturing he needs. Shouldn't it be the same for adults?

Here's a likely scenario: suppose a staff member goes to the director and asks, "May I work through my break and then leave early?" The director responds, "Sure." More of a conversation takes place between the director and the employee than we know, but the answer to the question "May I work through my break?" is "Yes."

Now the rest of the team sees that for the entire week, this other employee is working through her break and leaving early. You think to yourself, "I'm working hard. I'd like to work through my break. I'd like to leave early." Ever think that way? Sure, everyone does, but in this situation, you don't know whole story. You need to trust that the administration is going to help every person on the team in whatever way she needs to be helped. What you don't know is that the team member who is working through her break and leaving early has a husband who has just been diagnosed with cancer.

Keeping Your Team Strong

How do you keep you team strong? Helping each team member to balance work and life issues is a significant way to keep your team strong. You cannot park your problems at the door. The life you have outside of your program has made you who you are. Your collective life experiences, the good and the bad, forge your experience, tenacity, and drive. Every experience you've had outside the school doors has helped to create the good person you are inside those doors. You don't want to leave your life outside. You just want to make sure that you help someone when she has fallen out of formation.

At any given time, many on your team will be struggling with personal matters, like a broken car or water in the basement. Some may be struggling with big stuff like divorce, illness, or even the death of loved ones. Winning teams keep the safety of the children as their primary concern and simultaneously focus on helping every adult in their group. While taking care of other adults is your responsibility, it's also your responsibility to take care of yourself. That's step 4.

OPTIMIZE YOUR KNOWLEDGE

1 Why is it important to help others **balance** their life and work issues?

____

____

____

____

2 Explain why your director or supervisor **may not share** all the information about what is going on in the lives of other employees.

____

____

____

____

3 Without giving her name, describe how someone at work or in your family is struggling and then **plan a few steps** to help that person.

____

____

____

____

STEP 4

Take Care of Yourself

4

During work, I take time for myself to focus my thoughts and to renew my physical strength and mental outlook.

- Always
- Usually
- Sometimes
- Never

Do You Take Care of Yourself at Work?

It's likely you answered, "Occasionally" or "Never" to this question. You were probably thinking, "Do I take care of myself during work? Are you kidding? I barely have time to take care of me at home."

Time for Yourself at Work: Are You Kidding?

Why is it important to take care of yourself at work? In this fast-paced world, it's important to take care of yourself, period. Given the work you do with young children, being well rested, alert, and focused is a necessity. The safety of children lies in your hands. How can you take care of children well if you don't take care of yourself? Here's why you have to take care of yourself!

- The safety of the children and their well-being depends on you being well rested, alert, and focused.
- Caring for young children is a physically and emotionally demanding job, and you must take breaks throughout the day.
- Taking care of yourself is your responsibility. It is unlikely that anyone else will initiate this goal.
- In a winning team, each member is performing at her personal best. You cannot perform at your best if you do not take time to renew yourself.
- You probably become cranky and impatient with the children and adults you work with when you don't take care of yourself. And that's not good for anyone!
- A long-term commitment to the early childhood field and your team means taking care of yourself and working at a sustainable pace. Can you keep up your current pace for the next ten years?

What Can You Do to Take Care of Yourself at Work?

Think about the past week at work. Now write down the space below what you did last week or recently for yourself at work.

What I did at work to focus my thoughts and renew my physical strength and mental outlook.

____

____

____

Having trouble thinking of anything? That's not a good sign. Here are a few ideas to get you started: took a walk, read a book, went outside. Yes, the care of children is your first concern, and you must make sure that coverage is met before you leave the room. And true, you shouldn't be reading a book if you are supposed to be watching the children. I do believe that teachers have a sixth sense, but I've yet to meet a teacher who really has eyes in the back of her head. All right, can you think of something you did for yourself?

Here's what a group of teachers I recently worked with had to say. Why is the list so short? They weren't taking care of themselves very well either.

- Went for a walk around the school.
- Wrote a letter to a friend.
- Read a book.
- Ate my lunch in front of my laptop. (*This one doesn't count.)*
- Left the school and went to a park, to the mall.
- Took a short nap in the teacher's lounge.
- Gave myself a high five in the bathroom mirror. (*Love that one!*)

What Eventually Happens If You Don't Take Care of Yourself at Work?

Over time, not taking care of yourself can led to marginal performance, illness, obesity, reduced energy, and stress—and that's just what happens to you. If that doesn't sound bad enough, eventually the children in your care and the adults that you work with will suffer too. How's that? When you start to get burned out, you become cranky, impatient, and resentful and may even start to feel sorry for yourself. Not such good steps to a winning team.

Think about your past week again. Did you work through your break? Not taking your break hurts you and the kids—we already talked about that.

Sometime when you choose to work through a break, finish a lesson plan, clean out a closet, write daily sheets, or always volunteer to fill the coverage gap, you become angry. That doesn't seem to make sense given that you made a choice not to take your break. But here's how it goes: you start looking around, wondering why everyone else is not as committed and dedicated as you are. "Don't they care as much as I do?" They do care as much as you do, but they realize that to consistently perform well in the long run, to create a winning team, everyone needs a break.

Can you stand another goose story? When geese are flying in formation, every so often the lead goose leaves the head position and drops to the back of the line. Another goose moves into his place. Why? Because even geese need a rest. They take turns and make sure everyone gets a break. The same goes for early childhood education. That's why there is a staffing and coverage schedule that includes breaks and lunches: so the children are well supervised and every team member has a chance to renew her physical strength and mental outlook. Do you consistently take your break and lunch? You should.

No Coverage?

What do we do when there isn't coverage? What if you want to take your break or lunch but there just isn't coverage? Taking care of the children is priority number one, and there are times when there is nothing you can do. There are times when you will have to work through your break or stay a little longer. If lack of coverage is a continuing problem in your program, the administrators and you need to come up with ideas for a new plan. Always missing your break and lunch is not an option.

Try these ideas when coverage is not available:

- Take shorter breaks and lunches on a particular day, so everyone gets a rest.
- Combine classrooms for a short time.
- Have the administrators cover the room.
- Hire a floater to help with staffing gaps.
- Ask parents to help in the classroom under the supervision of a teacher.

Coverage is an ongoing issue in early childhood education, but if you want to keep that team running, you have to find creative ways to get out of the classroom and take your break.

A Trip to the Bathroom at Least?

Now a bit of a personal question: did you have to go to the bathroom sometime last week but didn't do so? I'll bet you respond yes to that question. It's a common behavior of teachers, this having to go but holding it. Common, yes. Good for you, no. Again, you don't want the children to ever be unattended, but if the least you can do to take care of yourself is go to the bathroom, please do so!

In a recent teacher training, I asked a group of teachers the same question: "How many of you had to go to the bathroom during work last week but didn't?" The room was filled with laughter. One teacher even admitted that she needed to go right now, during the training, and that she had been holding it all day. We excused her from the training.

At that workshop, I gave out a performance award to the teacher who had *held it and didn't go*. The award was titled Held It the Longest. Here's how the session went. "We're going to give John this special award called Held It the Longest. Isn't it great? This award is going to go in his staff portfolio. When it comes time to do his performance appraisal, the director is going to pull out the award and say, 'John, you have the most amazing control. I cannot believe how you can hold that bladder. Based on your ability to hold your bladder, I feel that a raise and promotion are necessary. Maybe you can teach a workshop for the other staff so they can learn to hold it too.'"

Are you likely to get a raise and a promotion by holding it? What do you get when you hold it? You get a bladder infection, and that's not fun. This isn't a crazy, extreme example of how people don't take care of themselves in early childhood education. Your award for Held It the Longest is below!

Held It the Longest

AWARDED TO

____

Who Will Take Care of Me If I Don't?

You learned in step 3 to appreciate the lives of others and to help them in times of need. If you have a winning team, you can count on your teammates to help you, too, when things get tough. But lots of issues in your life, like fatigue and irritability, can be prevented simply by taking care of yourself. You may not exercise on every break or eliminate eating lunch while you work, but you can start by taking care of some of your basic needs like urinating, breathing, eating, moving around. You are diapering, feeding, toileting, singing to people all day long, and you must take care of yourself if you want to take care of the children and your team.

22 Ideas to Take Care of Yourself

1 Learn to say no more often when asked to help or volunteer.

2 Take a walk.

3 Use the stairs.

4 Park further away from the building.

5 Put a piece of fruit in your bag.

6 Carry something to read (a book, a magazine, or an article).

7 Go to the bathroom when you must.

8 Sit down and eat lunch.

9 Make a list of the things you want to do.

10 Don't try to make everything perfect.

11 Close your eyes for a few minutes.

12 Meditate.

13 Stretch.

14 Call a friend to chat.

15 Write a letter to someone.

16 Plan a special outing, such as a movie or a manicure, that you can look forward to.

17 Give yourself a high five in the mirror.

18 Don't take life so seriously.

19 Watch the children play and learn from them.

20 Laugh more.

21 Listen to music.

22 Go outside.

Energy Zappers

On the road to caring for yourself, here are several ways that people often set themselves up to fail. Take a look at the list below and see if you are guilty of zapping yourself and your team.

Always saying yes to every request. Being a willing and dedicated team player doesn't mean you have to volunteer for every extra program project, always straighten up the staff lounge, or stay late to provide coverage. Know your energy level and what you can do without becoming too stressed out or ending up sick.

Trying to be a perfectionist. It is impossible to do things perfectly. Do your best with the resources, energy, and experience you have at the time. If every team member strives for excellence, you'll have an excellent team.

Not getting enough sleep. What do you get from lack of sleep? Impatience, frustration, and lack of focus. Cranky children are more likely to misbehave, and so are cranky adults.

Eating poorly. Skipping meals only makes us more likely to eat on the run, grab unhealthy snacks, and gorge ourselves later. Take time to eat breakfast and lunch. What's healthy? If you have a food service in your program, just look at the kid's menu, which should work for you too.

Forgetting to organize your day. Each day, make a list of the things you need to accomplish in your personal and work life. Include things like making appointments for doctors or home repair, closets you need to clean out at work, and calling a parent just to check in. You are less likely to get stressed and more likely to accomplish the things you want to do if you make a list.

winning ways

You can't take care of the children you teach, your coworkers, or even your own family if you don't take care of yourself. Oh, yes, you have heard that many times, but have you ever made yourself a priority? You should, and no one can take that initiative but you.

The next step to a winning team is about giving up the gossip. Are you ready for the challenge?

OPTIMIZE YOUR KNOWLEDGE

1 Would you receive the **Held It the Longest** award? Explain why that type of continued behavior can be detrimental to you and your team.

____

____

____

____

2 Call another program to ask how they deal with breaks and lunches when they are **short of staff coverage** and unable to meet required teacher-to-child ratios. Write their strategy here.

____

____

____

____

3 List three ways you would like to start **taking better care of yourself** and then prioritize those ideas.

1 ______________________________

2 ______________________________

3 ______________________________

STEP 5

Don't Gossip

5

I do not participate in gossip, and I speak directly to other adults with whom I have questions or issues.

- Always
- Usually
- Sometimes
- Never

Do You Gossip at Work?

How did you rate yourself? I'd like to say that I "Never" gossip, but that just wouldn't be true. You may try not to gossip, but somehow conversations tend to gravitate toward talking about other people. It's part of our human nature to notice what others are doing and to talk about them. The thing with that part of human nature is that people rarely talk about the good things that others are doing—you don't hear many conversations in the school parking lot or staff lounge that sound like this: "Did you see that amazing project she did with the children? I've never seen anyone with that much creativity. On top of that, her room is so organized, and she has a wonderful way of helping the parents in her class feel more at ease. I really wish I could be more like her. Don't you feel the same way? We should call and tell everyone what a great job she is doing."

That conversation doesn't sound very familiar, does it? How about this one: "Did you see that project she did with the children? It wasn't very organized, and you'd think she would know the children only want to play with the materials. I don't think she'll become the art teacher anytime soon! And did you see how messy her room is? I bet the parents don't know how things really are in that class. One of the parents in that class is a friend of mind. I should tell her how that teacher really is. It would be wrong of me not to. Don't you agree?"

Unfortunately, that's probably the conversation to which you can better relate. Yes, it's true: people are more likely to complain or say unfavorable things about others than to talk about their talents and accomplishments. Just look at the checkout aisle of any grocery store, and you'll see lots of magazines spouting all the bad things about celebrities. Somehow it tends to make us feel better when others are not doing so well.

Gossip Is Hurtful

It's wrong to gossip about others in any situation, but when you talk about members of your own team—your work family—you can really do some damage. You may notice that someone is not performing well. So what do you do? You respectfully and professionally mention this to the person and offer to help her. When someone is struggling, you don't want to have the attitude of "I caught you!" You want to have the attitude "I want to help you."

Remember that when one of your team members has a problem in any classroom, it's your problem too. If someone isn't performing well at your center, you may momentarily think, "That's not my class. My class is going great." It may not be your class, but it is your program, and that's a reflection of you as well. You may feel good by comparing yourself to those less successful, but that's not how a successful team performs. Geese don't fly in little groups.

What Is Gossip?

To have a winning team, do you need to be able to talk to each other about what you see and think? Absolutely! The key is to talk *with* someone, not *about* someone. What is gossip? **Gossip is saying something about someone else that you would not say directly to that person.**

The Definition of Gossip

Let's look at each section of that definition.

Gossip is saying something	*You are talking aloud, sending a text, writing an e-mail to a third party.*
About someone else	*You are talking about a person not included in the conversation.*
That you would not say	*You are not telling the person you are talking about what you think.*
Directly to that person.	*If you spoke directly to that person, she could explain, or change, or correct the problem.*

Why Do People Gossip?

Team members gossip for a number of reasons. As I said, it's human nature, but there are other reasons people gossip. Gossip is harmful regardless of why someone is gossiping, but sometimes if you know why a person is gossiping, you can help solve the problem and eliminate the gossiping. Take a look at the following list.

People gossip to make themselves feel better. Maybe a member of your team feels insecure or needs more attention.

People gossip in the absence of information. Sometimes when you don't have information, you speculate, wondering what children are moving up, who's getting a promotion, or why a parent is upset. Keep in mind that you don't need to know it all. You have to trust your administrators to give you the information you need to do your job.

People gossip because they are afraid to deal with a problem. It is certainly easier to complain than to actually talk to another person about solving a problem. Don't be afraid to confront someone if you have a legitimate issue.

People gossip because it's a habit. Saying not-so-nice things about people is easy to do. Developing the habit of encouraging and acknowledging the good works of others is more difficult. Give it a try. You'll be a few steps closer to a winning team.

People gossip because other people listen. A person who gossips is not too effective if no one is listening. The person who listens to gossip is just as responsible as the person who gossips.

How Do You Deal with Gossip?

There are several ways to deal with gossip, but only one is most effective. When you hear other members of your team gossip, you can choose to do one of four things:

Join In

Your first choice when you hear another person gossiping is to join in! Oh yeah, some of us fall victim to that! You hear something and then add, "She was that way with me too. I had a hard time working with her. I had to ask for a transfer—that's why I'm not working in her room now." Yes, you can join in. Does joining help? Everyone knows it doesn't—it just makes things worse. By joining in, you are validating the gossip's behavior, harming the work family member you are talking about, and not addressing the problem.

Here's what I know about people who gossip, if someone is gossiping *to* you, one day they will be gossiping *about* you. Just because you are on the receiving end of that gossip information today doesn't mean that tomorrow you won't be the topic of gossip.

Don't join in.

Listen But Don't Participate

By listening to the gossip but not participating, you aren't adding to it, and that's a good thing. Maybe you don't even agree with what the gossip is saying, but you are nonetheless guilty, because gossiping requires a listener. You might listen for a variety of reasons—you feel curious, you are uncomfortable leaving, or you don't know what to say. If someone were talking about you, wouldn't you want whoever was listening to defend you and help you? I would.

Walk Away

With choice three, you have a better strategy. You're not adding to the gossip or even listening to it, and by walking away, you stop the gossip circuit that was directed toward you. Walking away is a good first step for people who encounter gossip. While doing so does stop the gossip, walking away doesn't keep the gossip from finding a more willingly listener, and it certainly does not help solve the problem. If you truly feel that you cannot confront a gossip directly, speak to your supervisor about who was gossiping and what was said. Does that sound like tattling? If someone said something wrong or hurtful about someone in your family, wouldn't you do someone about it? Help your work family too.

Confront, Redirect, and Support the Gossipmonger

This is the most effective, yet difficult, way to deal with gossip. Here are the three actions you should take when gossip comes your way: confront, support, and redirect the gossipmonger. You might say, "By the way you are talking, you sound as if you really don't like the way she acted. You should tell her directly so she knows how you feel." Your statement may be a bit stronger, "I think it's unfair to talk about her when she is not here. You should tell her how you feel. Wouldn't you want to know if someone felt that way about you?" Either way, you are telling the gossipmonger to tell her concerns to the person she is complaining about, not you.

By confronting the gossipmonger, you validate her feelings of being upset and let her know that what she is doing is not okay. With redirection, you guide her to speak directly to the person she is gossiping about.

At this stage, a gossip may respond that she's tried that and it doesn't work or she's too afraid. "I've tried to talk to her, and she just doesn't listen." You can support her by saying, "Try again; it might work this time" or "If you really want this to change, you'll figure out a way to tell her" or even, "Maybe you should tell the director if you can't talk to her."

You might even support someone by saying, "I'll walk with you to talk to that person" or "I'll go with you to speak to the director." Your support is not intended to pair up and overpower the person being gossiped about, but to give the gossipmonger support. Many people are scared of confrontation. They can talk a big game and complain, but creating a winning team depends on everyone taking an active role in eliminating gossip and dealing with issues.

Confront

You let the person know that gossiping is not acceptable.

Redirect

You tell the person to speak directly to the person with whom she takes issue.

Support

You encourage your teammate to speak to that person even if she is afraid, feels as if it's pointless, or has already tried.

How Do You Know If You Are Gossiping?

You know the definition of gossiping—but how do you know if and when you are doing it yourself? Here are a few ways to tell. You are gossiping when you know that what you are saying is not constructive or helpful. When you know it's not true. When you get that feeling you are doing something that isn't right. Those are all ways to know you are gossiping, but here's the best one: suppose you are talking about another person to a team member and that person shows up. If you are gossiping, you are going to feel pretty uncomfortable about what you're saying. If you aren't gossiping, you should be able to turn to the person and say, "I was just talking about you to so-and-so, and here's what I was saying." Now, that's the true test!

How Do You Speak Directly to That Person?

This is the hardest part. When you have to tell someone something difficult, be honest, but speak from your heart. You might say, "This is really hard for me to say, but I wanted to let you know that I didn't like the way you spoke to me the other day." Before you speak, ask yourself the two questions from step 1: "Does it really matter?" and "How does it affect the children?"

Gossip Is a Performance Issue

As a team member, you are dedicated to helping one another and that includes encouraging every team player to speak directly to the persons with whom they have issues. If you are gossiping, you have a responsibility to give up the gossip. Deal with issues head-on and speak positively about others on your team. If you continue to gossip, early childhood education may not be the place for you. Good care and education for children depend on the honest and constructive communication of the adults who care for them.

Extremely Hurtful Information

If you hear information that you feel has the potential to harm the children, parents, or staff in your program, it is your responsibility to report that information to your state licensing authority and/or the police. You may also want to tell your director, although you are not obligated to do so. Someone may say, "I don't want you to tell anyone." Your response must be "I can't promise you that I won't tell anyone." Whether you know it to be true or not, share that knowledge with the correct authorities and the administrators so they can take steps to protect others. This type of information may include employee performance that involves hurting or shaming a child, use of illegal drugs, or threats to a person, place, or thing.

I personally have little tolerance for gossiping. As a past director of programs, I'll admit that a bad attitude and gossiping made me more frustrated and angry than any other staff performance issues. Bottom line: don't gossip and don't listen to gossip. Gossip is hurtful, undermining, and usually not even true. It tends to make those who don't feel good about themselves feel better at the expense of others. Winning teams don't talk **about** each other, they talk **to** each other. Give up the gossip and try using one of your other talents and skills.

The next step to a winning team is identifying and using the many strengths that each team member brings to the job.

OPTIMIZE YOUR KNOWLEDGE

1 In your own words, define what **gossip** is.

____

____

____

____

2 Name the **best way** to deal with gossip and explain why.

---

3 What happens to your team if you allow gossip to **continue**?

STEP 6

Share Your Talents

6

I share my own special skills and expertise with other adults.

- Always
- Usually
- Sometimes
- Never

How Do You Move from a Team to a Winning Team?

You know that a team is made up of people who are working toward a common goal. In early childhood education, that goal is caring for and educating children and their families. Individual job descriptions list the specific responsibilities each person needs to perform to accomplish that goal. When everyone is doing her job, you are working as a team.

But how do you move from just a team to a winning team? Before talking about how sharing your talents helps to create a winning team, it's worth listing some of the characteristics of a winning team:

- Everyone is passionate about her job.
- People are inspired to do more than just the minimal job requirements.
- Employees are encouraged to use their individual skills and talents to enhance the program.
- No one is afraid when one team member excels in a certain area, because people are given a chance to excel using their skills and talents.
- Employees are comfortable asking another team member who has a talent in a particular area to help them.
- People realize that each team member has something to contribute; they work together to name those talents and brainstorm ways to use them in the organization.

What Do You Have to Share?

Each person on a team has something to contribute, or she wouldn't be part of the team. Now, there are situations in which people choose not to use their skills and talents. For whatever reason, they don't want to work as part of a team. There are also situations in which a person may not have the skills it takes to work with young children. In both cases, these are performance issues that require the help of administrators.

Another common reason that people don't use their skills and talents to create a winning team is because their skills and talents haven't been identified. Even when you have identified your talents, you don't always think they can be used at work, that they can be applied to your job.

So let's find out what your skills and talents are. What do you do well? List below three things that you are good at doing. They needn't be work related: just think about what you like to do and do well. Here are some ideas to get you started. Are you a coupon clipper? Are you good at drawing? Are you good at gardening? Are you wonderful with animals? Do you just love to be with people? Do you love to organize? Are you good at writing? Are you a computer expert? Are you great with money or the lack thereof?

My Skills and Talents

1 ______________________________

2 ______________________________

3 ______________________________

Are you having trouble making that list? Unfortunately, many people have a difficult time naming their good qualities. I recently asked this same question during a school staff meeting, and one teacher replied, "I could tell you three things that I'm not good at doing." Do you feel like that? Sometimes it's easier for the people you work with to identify your talents than you. If you can't come up with a list on your own, ask one of your team members to write down your skills. Then you can begin to see all of the positive qualities others see in you.

Do You Have a Winning Attitude about Yourself?

Without a winning attitude, there can't be a winning team. Think about what the teacher said of her talents and skills: "I could tell you three things that I'm not good at doing." Now think about your work with children. Imagine that you couldn't think of anything good about a particular child; you could only list the things that were wrong with him. You don't think of kids that way, right? You look for the best. With some challenging children, you may have to dig a little deeper, but you always come up with something positive: "She's good at moving around." "He sure is a conversationalist." You look for the best in children, but you may not do that for yourself. Your team can't function without you. Do you realize that? You bring something special to the team. Now, go back and write down three things you are good at doing!

Here are some of the answers I heard at the staff meeting I attended.

- I love to organize spaces.
- I am good at teaching adults.
- I have a good sense of humor.
- I am good at shopping for discounts.
- I love to bake.
- I am a good cook.
- I am good at listening to others.
- I play the piano.
- I sing well.
- I can fix cars.
- I enjoy doing crafts.
- I like to set up parties.
- I have a collection of stamps.
- I really enjoy local history.
- I have a green thumb.

Share Your Talents at Work

Okay, you've identified what you are good at doing and what you enjoy doing, but what does that have to do with work? Some of those skills that you listed will help you to carry out your basic job responsibilities better, while others will help you to enhance your program and improve your team.

Here's the next step: share your talents at work. For some, that seems pretty easy. If you play the piano, you can play the piano for the children. If you bake well, you can bring in treats for the staff lounge. Okay, that's the idea, but you can do even more. More work? Hey, if it's something you love to do and you're passionate about, then it won't seem like work at all. Sharing your talents will not only help others but will also renew your enthusiasm for your job.

Here's my brainstorm list on the ways team members can share their talents at work. Add your ideas at the end of each category.

Cooking

- Cook with the children in your class.
- Start an enrichment activity and cook with other classes and age groups in your program.
- Cook treats with the children to use for a fundraiser.
- Make cookies with the children that the center can take to a local nursing home or other program.
- Make a center recipe book and give it as a holiday gift to parents or community neighbors.
- Conduct a child-and-parent cooking class.
- Make a special meal or snack for the parents and let the children serve it.
- Take the children on a field trip to the grocery store to buy the ingredients for a recipe.
- Write easy, kid-friendly recipes so others can cook with the children.
- ______________________________

Fix Cars

- Teach children about how cars work and move.
- Make small model cars with the children.
- Bring your own car to the center and let the children help you wash it, change the oil, or tinker with a cold engine.
- Visit a car dealership on a field trip to see different kinds of cars and how to fix them.
- Construct a life-size model car in your classroom.
- Make a map with the children of the streets around the center.
- Go on a field trip to a car wash.
- ______________________________

Now it's time to take your talents and brainstorm how you can share them at work.

Ideas to share my talents at work:

____

____

____

____

____

____

____

Sharing Your Talents at Work

How do you share your talents? First, you have to identify what they are. You can make a list of your skills and talents and ask other team members to identify your strengths. Next, brainstorm all the ways you can use your talents at work. Remember to think beyond your classroom.

Where, When, or How Can You Share Your Talents?

- In your classroom
- With another classroom
- With the whole center
- In an enrichment class
- For a classroom party
- For a center party
- For a staff party
- For a family party
- At a family meeting
- At a staff meeting
- For your corporate sponsor, if you have one
- In the community (a nursing home, hospital, or food pantry)
- With other centers in the area
- At a community college
- In a local school
- By writing an article to distribute or publish
- In your classroom newsletter
- In your center newsletter
- In your company newsletter (if you are multi-site)
- On your website
- At a workshop for your classroom, or center, or at a conference

Get Out of Your Comfort Zone

The list of how and where you can share your talents is endless. Remember: as a member of the early childhood field, you have a team that extends far beyond your program doors. It is your responsibility as a professional and as a member of a winning team to share the successful ways you have found to care for and educate young children with others in the industry. Creating good ideas and working with the children are what you do well. Taking your talents and center successes and sharing them on local, state, and national levels, may feel overwhelming and a bit scary. Nevertheless, push yourself to move beyond your comfort zone. Give a workshop for others. Start small by just reading about or demonstrating your talent to your follow teachers, then try to share it with the whole center; eventually move to other programs. If you don't feel comfortable talking in front of others, give it a try, but also consider recording your presentation to show others or taking photographs and writing captions.

Tips for Sharing Your Talents at Work

- Know that everyone has special skills and talents.
- In addition to those talents typically considered, such as playing a musical instrument or singing, identify less conventional skills, such as organization, speaking a second language, and carpentry.
- If seeing your own talents is difficult for you, ask another team member or your supervisor to help you discover them.
- Make a plan for how you can share your talents to enhance your program and your team. Start with small, attainable goals and stretch yourself to share your talents with a larger audience.
- Remember that sharing your talents at work is not an extra job. To create a winning team, you have to give your personal best.
- When you are excited and passionate about what you do, everyone around you benefits. That goes for good organization. Everybody loves a clean closet! Few can keep it that way.

Although members of your team may have different responsibilities and different accountability, everyone on a winning team is equally important. Your team can't function without you, and you can't function for very long without your team. In a winning team environment, your contributions to the program include not only your primary job responsibilities but also how you choose to share the talents. You may be responsible for organizing field trips, scheduling coverage, decorating the lobby, or mentoring new teachers. How are you going to share your talents? You are a completely unique person whose gifts are like no one else's.

Now turn your attention to step 7, Be a Problem Solver.

OPTIMIZE YOUR KNOWLEDGE

1 Name five characteristics of a team that **works well** together.

1 ________________________

2 ________________________

3 ________________________

4 ________________________

5 ________________________

2 When team members use their **skills and talents**, even jobs at the same level, for example, teacher assistant, may look different. Is that okay? Why or why not?

____

____

____

____

3 **Interview** someone who works closely with you or knows you well. Ask that person to identify three things you do well. Are those traits consistent with your own assessment of your skills and talents, or are they different?

1 ________________________

2 ________________________

3 ________________________

STEP 7

Be a Problem Solver

7

Without being asked, I help others by proposing and carrying out creative solutions and improving problematic situations.

- Always
- Usually
- Sometimes
- Never

Are You a Problem Solver?

If you think about your classroom team or the group of people with whom you work most closely, I'll bet you can rate yourself as "Always" or "Usually." Now, think about the entire center. It's easy to remark, "I'm glad that's not my classroom," when others have to deal with problems like marginal teacher performance, spirited children, or demanding parents. Are you a problem solver for the whole center or just your classroom? Most people think that dealing with centerwide issues is the job of the administrators. But not on a winning team. Let's look at the difference.

From Classroom Team to Center Team

In most programs, there are teams working within teams. Groups of adults work in different classrooms, usually with different ages of children. You have people working in administration, food service, and building maintenance. Those are all teams with common jobs. Although the information here applies to and should be used and perfected by each small team, your larger goal is to create a winning team by moving beyond your classroom and viewing the entire center staff as your team.

What Steps Do You Need to Take to Move from Classroom Team to Center Team?

People often think that getting their classroom teams in place takes precedence over working on a centerwide team. Actually, that's not true. You should be doing both simultaneously, because having a winning center team gives each classroom access to more ideas, help, support, and encouragement. Everyone can use more of that!

Changing your perspective from classroom team to center team requires a new way of thinking. Here are some concepts to consider.

Everyone is hired to work for the program, not a particular job, age group, class, or shift. You may have more experience working with a particular age group or want a certain schedule to balance your own work and life. A winning team takes these personal preferences into account when assigning jobs and making the schedule, but you all work for the program and should be willing to change diapers in the infant room even if you are the kindergarten teacher. That's what a winning team does.

Every problem that occurs in the program is the problem of the whole team. "I'm glad it's not my room" is a comment that doesn't work on a winning team. When a classroom team or a group of employees is struggling, the whole center is responsible for helping.

The actions of each individual team member reflect upon the entire team. When you work in early childhood education, you are a role model for the children and the field, whether you are at work or home. If a member of your team is impatient and rude at a local restaurant during lunch, it's likely that others will think the whole staff is like that. Caring for children is a serious job. Ask yourself if the choices you make at the center, in the community, and in your personal life represent your program well.

You help every team member succeed. You help every child succeed; the same goes for adults. Never give up on an adult. Exhaust all your resources by trying to help that person. Ultimately the choice to succeed lies in the hands of that individual, but you can do your part. There will be times when everyone needs help. Caution—goose story coming! When a goose falls out of formation, other geese come to the rescue.

You share the failures and mistakes of your program and work together to prevent them from happening again. Learn from your program's mistakes. Solving a problem is an opportunity to work more closely as a team while improving the school's program. If you really learn from your mistakes, it's unlikely that you will make the same mistake again.

You share and celebrate the successes of your program. Working with young children is a tough job. Enjoy the big and small successes of your program. Think of all the things you have to celebrate: hiring a new teacher, helping a child transition to a new room, doing a new project, working together. The list is endless. It's your choice to see the positive side or not.

There is not one job on your team that is more important than another job. It takes us all to get it done. Don't assume that one job is any easier or harder than another. Do what you are supposed to do and help others along the way.

What Should a Problem Solver Do?

Being a center problem solver is not a license to get into everyone's business or be the center's know-it-all. On the contrary, as members of a winning team, everyone has the same job when it comes to problem solving.

- Be willing to help with a problem, even when it is not in your room or you didn't cause it. "It's not my problem" is not the attitude or the answer.
- Offer to help another classroom or area of the program. Don't wait for someone to ask you.
- Do not judge those who are involved in the problem. Simply work to help them.
- Realize that even though everyone owns the center's problems, not everyone will be called to solve them. Due to confidentiality and need-to-know, you may be unaware of many issues, especially if you work in a large program.
- Trust your administrators to tell each person what she needs to know to help with the problem.
- Maintain confidentiality yourself.
- Appreciate the opportunity to help, whether you are providing staffing coverage so other adults can meet or you are actively working through the issue. Both kinds of help are important.

Barrier Spotter or Hurdle Jumper?

As humans, we readily judge and criticize other adults, especially when those adults are experiencing problems. It's common to hear things like "No wonder the parent is mad at her for losing her child's gloves. That teacher is so unorganized I'm surprised she didn't lose all the gloves." If you're on a winning team, you want your program to succeed. If you know a teacher has organizational challenges, shouldn't you help her before there is a problem?

How about this example: "I knew lunch was going to be late today. It always is when we have grilled cheese. Now all the toddlers are crying." Who loses out in this situation? The crying toddlers. If you know that lunch is late when it's grilled cheese, couldn't you get extra help in the kitchen on that day, serve something else, give the toddlers a more substantial snack that day, or not sit the toddlers at the table until the lunch arrives? There are a number of ways to deal with that issue. Help where you can, and speak up to fix a problem before it unfolds.

Barrier Spotter

If asked I you to write down all the things that bother you about your program or the things that are problems, you could probably write pages. I call the issues people complain about, the roadblocks that prevent new ideas, and the stumbling blocks that keep problems from being solved *barriers*. If you are always complaining, always saying, "That will never work" or "We already tried that before" and do not move on to solving the problem, then you are a barrier spotter. Barrier spotters can point out the worst of everything and the downside to all good ideas. Barrier spotters can point out every problem, but they do not make efforts to help solve it. Are you a barrier spotter?

Hurdle Jumper

Being a barrier spotter isn't a bad thing if it enables you to prevent problems before they occur or to point out elements of the program that need improvement. In those cases, you spot a barrier and move on to jump over it—you are a hurdle jumper. A hurdle jumper is determined, no matter how difficult a problem may be, to find a solution, to be a problem solver. A hurdle jumper sees solutions before problems even occur. When a child places a full cup of juice near the edge of the table, a hurdle jumper moves the juice closer to the center of the table and says, "Let's move your cup so it doesn't fall." When a hurdle jumper sees a teacher who is struggling, she steps in to help, even when it's not her room. Are you a hurdle jumper?

Barrier Spotter	Hurdler Jumper
"With the third teacher out, we won't get our breaks today."	"If we ask the room next door for help, we can all take a break."
"The director never offers to help in the room when we need her."	"Let's call the director to see if she can help us."
"That parent forgot to bring in gloves for her child again."	"We have some extra gloves today, and I'll call her mom at lunch."
"We don't have enough glue to do our art project."	"Today the children can use tape, and we can buy glue tomorrow."

How to Be a More Effective Problem Solver

- When you see a problem or potential problem, address it immediately. Don't wait for things to become worse.
- Forget the attitude "It's not my problem." If it's happening in your program and you work there, it's your problem.
- Don't be afraid to speak up. Wouldn't you want someone to tell you?
- Determine what the problem is. Often when people are emotionally upset, they need help identifying what the problem really is. Name the problem and start helping to solve it.
- Determine what you want to happen. Moving away from what is happening to what you want to happen is problem solving. Make sense?
- Write down the problem and what you want to happen. Putting things on paper forces you to focus more closely on the issue.
- Believe that there is a legitimate problem inside every complaint. Some issues may seem meaningless, and the way in which someone explains the problem may be emotionally wrought, but usually a legitimate issue can be found behind every complaint.
- Ask questions to better understand the problem. What you see may not be what is happening.
- Work with a group of people to solve a problem. Everyone brings a different perspective, advice, and experience.

Living With It

Sometimes solving a problem doesn't mean changing the situation but learning to live with it. You can't live with situations that are harmful or hurtful to children or adults, but you can improve, enhance, or develop a new way to deal with the problem. Here's what I mean. Suppose there is a column in the gross-motor area of the facility and you are concerned about children bumping into it. You can't take the column down because the building would collapse, so you have to live with it. But you can cover the column with a carpet or other protective covering. So you live with it but improve it. Make sense?

PROBLEM-SOLVING EXERCISE

What is the issue? (The problem) ______________________________

____

What do you want to happen? (The expectation) __________________

____

How can you make it happen? (The solution) ____________________

____

Brainstorm and list your ideas in these four categories:

Quick fix: ____

____

Short term: ____

____

Long term: ____

____

Living with it: ____

____

Problem Solving in a Small Group: Path to Success

Try this strategy for developing a better team approach to problem solving. Ensure that

- All the information about the problem is presented before solutions are discussed
- Others listen without interrupting
- Everyone has an opportunity to ask questions to better understand the issue
- The group suggests many solutions
- The group agrees upon a strategy

8 Problem-Solving Tips

1. Have one person verbally share the problem at hand.
2. Others in the group just listen until the person finishes. The listeners may not interrupt until the person is finished, but they can jot down a note or question for later.
3. If others in the group have additional information to share, they may do so when the first person finishes. They can add information at this time but not ask questions.
4. When all the information is presented, the listeners may ask clarifying questions to better understand the issue.
5. The people who shared the information answer others' questions.
6. The listeners then share their suggestions and ideas.
7. The person who shared the problem listens and adds her own ideas.
8. The group records all the ideas and develops a strategy for solving the problem.

Being a problem solver is more than just pointing out a problem. If you are a team player, you are constantly identifying ways to improve and enhance your program. As you recognize situations, policies, or facilities issues that need your attention, think about what's not happening well, but more important, think about what should be happening. As I mentioned, it's much easier to complain about circumstances than to fix them. Being a barrier spotter is fine. It's important to always address way to improve your program. Finding a way to move past those problems, becoming a hurdle jumper, is even better. Can you make the leap? What's the next step? Arrive on Time is step 8.

OPTIMIZE YOUR KNOWLEDGE

1 **What do you think** about the following statement from this step: "Everyone is hired to work for the program, not a particular job, age group, class, or shift."

2 Explain the **difference** between a hurdle jumper and a barrier spotter.

3 Name a problem **you solved** recently at work or in your personal life. Analyze what you think you did well and what you would do differently in the future.

STEP 8

Arrive on Time

8

I am prepared for work by being on time.

- Always
- Usually
- Sometimes
- Never

Do You Get to Work on Time?

How did you rate yourself? There's not a common answer for this step, but there is a common expectation: arrive on time. Step 8, Arrive on Time, could be really short. Here's what you need to know: consistently be on time or find another job. Too tough? Not really. Regardless of your personality, your family life, or the reliability of your transportation, you can only create a winning team by requiring that everyone arrives on time. No exceptions.

Will There Be Times When You Are Late?

Now, are you occasionally going to be late? Yes, most people will be late a few times over the course of their career. Some people are never, ever late, even when it snows or floods. I think they must live at the center. But most people will be tardy at some time. Why? A number of reasons: traffic is unpredictable, people get sick, and things happen in your life. If you are a parent yourself, you know. As a working mom of four, the minute I got in my car to go to work, somebody would pee in their pants or throw up. You never know what will make you late. It doesn't really matter why you are late. Some excuses seem more legitimate than others, but your absence at the center is felt in the same way.

There are some very serious reasons that may keep you from work, such as illness, accident, or death of a loved one. In those situations, don't worry. Others will cover for you; they'll make it work. That's what a winning team does!

Frequently Late?

So yes, there will be times when you are late. But if you are perpetually late, you must change that or you find a new profession. Being late in this field just doesn't work, because no matter how fabulous you are as a teacher or employee, you can't make up for the time you've missed at the center. You weren't there, and that means coverage was off and children didn't have as much attention as they deserved.

Why Is Being on Time So Important?

Why is it so important to be on time? That seems pretty obvious: there are a certain number of children, a set teacher-to-child ratio, and a staffing schedule that ensures those ratios are met. Right? But so often I hear directors excuse a tardy teacher by saying, "But she's such a good teacher."

Everyone likes good teachers, but let's look at it like this. Does anyone need a substitute teacher? That would be a unanimous yes. Okay, I'm willing to apply for the position. I have many years of experience, I'm a hard worker, and I even train other teachers. I'm a pretty good teacher. Would you hire me? You'd probably say, "Sure." But what if I were always late? You see, it doesn't matter if someone is a good teacher or not if she is always late. I would rather work with a teacher who is always on time and learning to be a good teacher than a master teacher who is always late. Who would you choose for your winning team?

The concept of punctuality is uniquely important to early childhood education. Challenge me on this statement, but I think this is the only industry, with the exception of medical triage professionals, for which being on time is so important. In early childhood education, enough adults must be present for the number of children present. When you are late, you bring down the whole team. And when you are late and the director doesn't do anything about it, one of two things usually happens. Either other employees start being late because they know there are no consequences for tardiness, or the rest of the team gets angry because one teacher is allowed to be late and the others are not.

Do Administrators and Directors Have to Be on Time?

Administrators and directors are responsible for the center at all times, whether they are in the building or not, just as you are responsible for what happens in your classroom even when you are not there. Most good directors work way too many hours and are probably at the center too much. They actually need to take time for themselves. Remember step 4, Take Care of Yourself?

But do they need to be on time? If they have committed to a certain schedule or have a meeting or a tour planned, yes. It's not okay for directors to pop in and out during center hours without someone knowing where they are and how to get in contact with them. Why? Being on time is respectful and professional even for those who don't work in a classroom and as supervisors of the program, they are responsible for their teams.

You have to encourage your director to leave on time if she seems to be spending too much time at the school. If she's helped to develop a winning team, you can fly without her for a bit while she takes a break and falls out of formation. (Had to slip a goose story in there.)

Not Prepared, Not on Time

All right, we've established that you have to be on time, but are you running through the parking lot with wet hair and a cup of coffee, just sliding through the center's doors as your shift begins? Little hint: that's not on time. On time is being prepared to work in the classroom or at your job when you are scheduled. On time means that you've gone to the bathroom, taken off your coat, washed your hands, and are ready to start working.

Here's what it takes to be on time and prepared:

- Be well rested.
- Be professional in appearance (no wet hair).
- Arrive at the school before you have to be in the classroom or at your position.
- Deal with personal issues.
- Turn off your cell phone.
- Put away personal belongings such as your coat and handbag.
- Use the restroom.
- Finish any food or drink you may have.
- Wash your hands.
- Be mentally present.
- Put on a smile.
- Bring a good attitude.

There's more about each of these in *Winning Ways for Early Childhood Professionals: Being a Professional.*

Always Running Late?

It's never anyone's intention to be late. Most people are just so busy and have so many things to organize that looking for the last thing they need to get out of the door causes them to be late. For me, this sometimes means I'm looking for one of my children.

Everyone tries to be better organized, but one of the greatest challenges of the day is just getting out of the house in the morning. Do you have that problem? Use these ideas as a way to arrive on time.

Prepare as much as possible the night before. This tip really works. It's always more difficult to find things in the morning when you are under a time constraint and stressed. Set the automatic coffeepot, pack your lunch, and set out your clothes for the next day or even for the entire week. Include the underwear, socks, shoes, even hair accessories and jewelry.

Keep the same stuff in the same spot. By keeping things in the same spot, your actions become habit and you are less likely to lose things. Place the things you are taking with you the next morning by the door. Write a note, or put your purse or car keys next to what to take from the refrigerator.

Get up earlier if you're always running late. A few extra minutes of sleep may seem like the best way to cope with the morning rush, but those minutes can make the difference between hectic and hurried. There are some who no matter how early they get up still run late.

Get going even if you are running early. Many people start out early and then add an extra chore or activity like folding a load of laundry or watching TV, which causes them to be late.

Have a consistent morning routine. Adults and children function better when they know what to expect. If your consistent morning routine is what is getting you into tardy trouble, change it.

Rush out the Door or Enjoy Unhurried Time?

In the morning, there's a lot to do in a short amount of time. Some people pop out of bed, quickly conquer the morning, and head out the door. Others need to wake up slowly, enjoy some leisure time, and have unhurried moments. Which type of morning person are you?

Your life is full of tasks, at home and at work. Getting organized and planning ahead is the only way to meet all your responsibilities. You can make lots of excuses about being late, and yes—being on time is difficult. Will you occasionally be tardy? Probably, but the goal is always to arrive on time or be early. Your team and your job depend on it! Learn more on how to get organized in step 9.

OPTIMIZE YOUR KNOWLEDGE

1 Why is being on time so crucial in early childhood education?

____

____

____

____

2 Name three things you or someone else can do to avoid often being late.

1 ______________________________

2 ______________________________

3 ______________________________

3 Do you think the director of a program should terminate an employee for habitually being late? Evaluate the possibilities.

STEP 9

Get Organized and Return Things You Borrow

9

I organize my workspace and share my resources with other adults. I respect the workspace of other adults by asking before I borrow something and by returning it when I am finished.

- Always
- Usually
- Sometimes
- Never

Organized—Are You Kidding?

Step 9 has two components, one about organizing your workspace and the other about returning the things you borrow. Just a little hint: when you are organized and prepared, you don't have to borrow as many things. When you don't have to borrow as many things, you don't have to return as many things.

Early childhood educators tend to like stuff: stuff you buy, stuff you find on sale, stuff you get off the side of the road, just stuff. And the reason you have so much stuff is because you're so creative. You can use the stuff to help children make life-sized igloos from plastic milk containers, do an entire science experiment with empty toilet paper rolls, and make just about anything from wallpaper samples.

The problem with lots of stuff is that it tends to make a mess, and your excitement about creativity may be far greater than your drive for organization. Yes, there are a few organizational geniuses and clean freaks around, but even those who aspire to a neater workspace have little time, given the constant busyness of this field.

Are You Organized?

Imagine you are planning to do a cooking project with the children. You are getting the ingredients together only to find out that you have everything you need except the sugar. You are making cookies, and substituting salt for sugar just won't do. Are you organized? Yes, if you are collecting the materials the day before you plan to do the activity. Are you organized if you are collecting the materials right before the activity? No.

But what if you are the type of person who can throw everything together at the last minute and it just seems to work out? Salt, no sugar, no problem. We'll do an activity about how salt and sugar look alike, and how if you interchange them, the cookies taste different. How's that for creativity? That's fine for some, some of the time, but often there needs to be a more detailed plan. You need better organization.

To create a winning team, you have to develop an organizational style that works for you and the people around you. That can be hard. Let's define organization and then look at people's organizational personalities.

WHAT IS ORGANIZATION?

So what is organization? The simple, basic answer is being able to quickly find the things you need to get the job done. Do you have the items that you need to care for and educate children, to do your job? Are they close at hand? Sometimes people think that aspiring to a color-coded filing system with typed labels in plastic sleeves is the only way to get organized. For some important things in your program, such as the children's files and staff files, that might be the best approach, but there's no right way to get organized, only an approach that creates a safe environment and works well for your team.

What Does Organized Look Like?

- The environment is safe and clean.
- Employees can quickly find the things they need to do their job.
- The things they need are plentiful and at their fingertips.
- The organizational style of each individual is acceptable to the team.
- The organizational style of the team meets the criteria of state licensing, accreditation, corporate values (if employer-sponsored), and company goals and policies, if a multi-site program.

What's Your Organizational Personality?

Are you organized, messy, or somewhere in between? Think about your home right now. Is your bed made? Is your bed unmade? Some people never make their beds. They figure, "Who sees it?" and they're just going to get back in it. Some always make their beds; they just can't leave the house without doing it. I always make my bed. It's just something that's a habit. I even make my bed when my husband is still in it. I just make it over him!

Let's try another question. How many of you don't mind a big ol' set of dirty dishes in your sink? How many of you immediately wash the spoon and bowl from your morning cereal and put them in the drying rack? There are some who do the dishes when they run out of clean ones and there are some who would never leave a dirty dish in the sink. My mother washes your dishes while you are still eating. If you put your glass down at my mother's house, she'll whisk it away and wash it. Anybody like that? In case you were wondering, I do leave dirty dishes in the sink.

Closer to Clean

Wouldn't you think that the people who made their beds never have dirty dishes in the sink and the people who don't make their beds have dirty dishes? That's not always the case. What's an organizational priority in our lives can be different for each of us. Some are very organized, some think they are organized, and some are just more laid back. For those of us who are just a bit too clean—taking the cup before someone drinks—and for those who are just a bit too relaxed—"Why wash a cup when you can buy a new one?"—the meeting place needs to be somewhere near the middle, but closer to clean.

You also have to remember that the organizational personality or standard you apply to your home is not necessarily the one that works well in your program. You need to have professional workspaces for yourself and the children that meet the standards of many groups. Do you organize your workspace to meet the standards set by and for your program? Does your workspace

- meet state licensing requirements;
- pass accreditation standards;
- represent corporate values, if employer-sponsored;
- meet company goals and policies, for multi-site programs;
- reflect the personal preference of the program leadership and staff;
- look professional;
- seem kid-friendly; and
- appeal to parents and prospective parents?

So the organization of your workspace needs to be one in which all the team members can quickly get the things they need to do their job, but it also needs to be safe, aesthetically pleasing, and professional.

What Makes a Winning Team Crazy?

Teams often argue about stuff. "Whose stuff is it?" "Where does the stuff go?" "Who is responsible for organizing the stuff and who replenishes the stuff?" What matters to one person is far different from what matters to another.

What if I were to display a child's artwork by taping it on the wall with a piece of masking tape that I tore off the roll? The strip of masking tape is showing and the artwork is crooked. Does that make you crazy? Do you need to fix it right away? That crooked, taped-up artwork bothers many people, while others won't see anything wrong with it. Is the way I hung the artwork okay? No, even if it doesn't bother me, it's still not professional. What if a child hung the picture that way? Then that's okay, and you can even add a sign to let others know that this is the work of a child.

How Stuff Can Make You Crazy

Here's the point, as a team, you can get into a lot of unnecessary arguments about organization. Here's the scoop:

1. The center should be homelike, but it is not your home, so be a little neater if you need to be.
2. If you like your workspace perfectly clean, don't expect the same from others. Strive for excellence and meet the standards of the various groups that govern your program.
3. Be flexible.
4. If you like to clean, don't be upset if others merely meet the cleaning standards.
5. If something is making you crazy, tell the person responsible. An open space or empty counter top is not an invitation to put your stuff there. All the stuff needs a place, preferably a labeled place.

Do You Return the Things You Borrow?

The second part of step 9 is "I respect the workspace of other adults by asking before I borrow something and by returning it when I am finished." Isn't that a novel idea? Returning what you borrow?

Think of the holiday coming up next. Thanksgiving? Valentine's Day? If the next holiday is Valentine's Day, would you store, or more accurately, hide red construction paper somewhere in your classroom? Why would you hide red construction paper? Yes, there are many hearts to be made, but are you afraid that you won't get any red construction paper if you don't hide it or that someone else in the school will take it all or take too much?

When you feel as if you must hoard supplies or take things without asking, or worse, not return them, then you are not working as part of a winning team. A winning team shares the red construction paper, and no one has to be afraid that others won't! Taking things from your team members without asking is not only rude and unprofessional, it's really considered stealing. We just prefer the word *borrow*.

When You Don't Return What You Borrow

Imagine someone is working in the front office and she reaches for the stapler, but it's not there. When you work in the office, not having the stapler at hand is like changing a dirty diaper in the infant room only to find that someone took the wipes. Not pleasant. Borrowing without asking is serious. It's one of the things that frustrates us and aggravates everyone on a team.

I just want everybody to know, in case your parents didn't tell you, you may not take stuff that is not yours, and if you take someone's stuff, you need to give it back. More important, you should say something like "May I borrow that?" Now I realize that in the throes of a busy day in early childhood education, you may want to grab things to get the job done. If your room is organized, well stocked, and you're prepared, you are less likely to need to grab anything. You have it all at your fingertips. That's organization! An organized winning team should practice these principles:

1. Respect each other's property.
2. Ask before borrowing something.
3. Know that if an item is tied to a string, you probably are not supposed to take it far.
4. Return the item, and replenish or replace it if you use it all.
5. Share your things willingly.
6. Know that most of the things in each classroom belong to the center. Sharing and switching things around gives a winning team more resources.
7. Don't hide goodies such as toys and puzzles in the closet. Rotate the materials to keep the children's interest, but don't hoard them. That doesn't help the children.

Tips on How to Clean Up Your Workspace

Share or Throw Out What You Don't Use

Have a toy and stuff swap. Have everyone in the program gather the toys and other items that they don't use and put them in a common place. Let everyone choose from the pile. What is trash to one teacher may be a treasure to another. Donate, recycle, or toss the leftovers.

Divide Your Classroom into Areas

If tackling your whole room to get rid of things seems too overwhelming, start with a drawer or cabinet. If you don't have the benefit of cleanup time without children, organize one area each day until the room is clean. Remember learning-center, teacher, food-service, and toileting and diapering areas. Make a list and check off the work you accomplish. Getting organized feels good!

Make Daily Cleanup Easier

Have a bin for dirty toys, bibs, and such. Place a photograph and word label on each bin to help children join in the cleaning. If possible, straighten up the room before moving to a new activity.

Have Staff Do a Thorough Cleanup Before Leaving for the Day

No one likes to come back to a messy room. Make cleaning a habit by creating a checklist of what needs to be done at the end of each day.

Is Organizing Worth the Effort?

Some good organizational efforts should make your life less hectic, and everyone can use that!

The Secrets of Organized Early Childhood Professionals

Sometimes other classrooms in the program look so neat that you often wonder, "Do they really teach kids?" "Do they spend all their time cleaning?" Organized people typically have a place for everything, and more important, they actually put things back after they've used them. What's really annoying is that they've taught the children in their classroom to do the same. Check out some of the secrets of organized early childhood professionals:

Have a "when you come in the classroom" routine for you and the children. It's much easier to be organized and stay organized when you make putting things in their place a priority and a habit. When you come into the classroom, put your things away as you go. Hang up your coats and put center mail in a bin to read and file later.

Keep countertops clutter-free. A workspace always looks neater and more appealing when it has clear spaces.

Less is more. The less you have, the less you have to organize. Workspaces look cleaner with less clutter. Remember the tips to clean your workspace and have out only what you and the children need. Get rid of things you don't use.

Use baskets or other containers for catch-alls and quick cleanups. Try to put things away as you work. If you find random toy pieces or others things, have a small basket at your work station to temporarily house them. Clean out the basket each day before you leave work.

Frame, laminate, or cover with contact paper any papers that must be posted all the time. Nothing is messier than yellowed, dog-eared papers hanging throughout your workspace. If you like to hang cards or letters from children, staff, or parents, use a central location.

Use cabinet doors or fabric to conceal storage spaces. Even if your storage areas are neatly organized, your workspace still looks cleaner when things are out of sight.

winning ways

There's no right way to get organized, but there are certain safety and program standards that you must abide by. Whether you are organizationally challenged or super neat, living with others in a place that is safe, functional, and aesthetically pleasing requires you to put things where they belong, clean up after yourself, and return things you borrow. Remember, if it's tied to a string, you're not supposed to take that item further than the length of the string. And if it's scissors on the string, using them to cut the string is a real no-no. When you respect others people's stuff, they are more likely to respect yours. On to step 10, Don't Judge Others.

OPTIMIZE YOUR KNOWLEDGE

1 Define what **organization** means to you.

____

____

____

____

2 Observe your classroom environment and note the areas that require **greater** organization.

____

____

____

____

3 From question 2, choose one of the areas in your room that requires greater organization and **draw a design** of how to improve the space.

STEP 10

Don't Judge Others

10

I talk with other adults in real conversations about what they are doing and thinking and do not judge but try to understand.

- Always
- Usually
- Sometimes
- Never

Do You Judge Others?

It's so easy for us to judge others. We do it almost instantly. You look at people's clothes, listen to the way they talk, watch their expressions and gestures, and then form a mental judgment of who they are and what they must be like. Interestingly enough, I bet most of us don't do that when we meet children for the first time. Somehow, in early childhood education you tend to see the good in the little ones you meet. You see their potential despite the way they may be dressed or how they talk. You just see children. Wouldn't it be great if you could just see adults, view adults as you view children? Think about how much better your team could function if you accepted adults for who they are and encouraged the potential in each of them.

Think about the adults with whom you have worked. When you first met them, did you ever think there were people you were not going to get along with? Did you ever meet someone whom you didn't like simply because you had already formed conclusions about the person for no reason except your initial biased judgment? "I don't think we'll work well together," you thought, only to find out that she wasn't anything like you imagined. She was one of the best people you ever worked with, and you actually became friends. Sound familiar? Your judgment was totally unfair.

If you judge others without even trying to know them better and appreciate their lives, they probably judge you that way too. What a shame. Think of all the missed opportunities. Wouldn't you want the benefit of people getting to know you through your actions and your work performance instead of by being judged? Of course you would.

How Do We Judge Others Unfairly?

People judge others in many ways. We judge them by

- Making assumptions based on how they look, talk, or gesture
- Using generalizations to categorize them
- Not being open to getting to know them
- Being unable to see or look for the often hidden potential in them

Have you ever worked with a person for a long time only to find out something about her that you never knew and that surprised you? "I didn't know she had a special-needs child of her own." "I didn't know she lost her husband to cancer." "I didn't know she grew up in a family like mine." Did it make you feel differently about the person? Did it make you feel bad that you weren't as nice to the person as you could have been or that you had judged her? I think everyone has experienced that. So what do you do? Try not to judge others.

Everyone Has a Story

Do you need to know everything about another person to have a good work relationship? No, but everyone has a story, so seek to understand, appreciate, and value other team members instead of judge them. Do you have to be friends with everyone you work with? Of course not, but you should be friendly with everyone you work with. When you appreciate others and try to better understand them, your life is enriched and your team wins.

How Do You Try to Understand Instead of Judge People?

Moving away from judging others demands a conscious change in thinking. It's easy to judge others for a variety of reasons. To create a winning team, you must push past those initial perceptions and try to get to know each other better. The funny thing about judgments is that they are often hard to overcome. You may have worked with someone for many years and carried an incorrect or partial understanding of her. Start having real conversations with other adults about what they are doing and thinking. Try to understand and not judge others. Here's how to get started:

Express Genuine Interest in Others. It's hard to motivate or encourage people when you don't really know them. What's the best way to get to know someone? Ask questions about the person—get her talking.

Follow Up with What You Learn. Remember what the person told you, and ask her about it the next time you talk. "Did you find a new apartment?" "How did it go with the family reunion this weekend?" Send a card or note to acknowledge successes or struggles in her life. Share information you come across that might interest her: names of good restaurants that offer certain foods or a list of events happening at the library.

Acknowledge people and refer them to others. Acknowledging people gives them affirmation and really makes them feel like members of the team. "Brielle got a puppy a few months ago. She might have some puppy items she is no longer using and a few ideas. I'll ask her for you." "If you are looking for good ideas to do with the children for the fall, Shanti is really creative. You should ask her."

Ask team members for their advice. Doesn't it feel great when someone respects you enough and thinks that your opinion is valuable enough to ask your advice? You probably have an informal group of people on your team to whom you usually confide and whom you ask for advice. Expand that group. Ask someone for advice whom you have never asked before.

Do something unexpected for someone on your team. Fill his in-box with notes of praise. Slip a gift card in his coat pocket. Clean up the art project before he gets a chance. Being noticed by others draws you closer to the team. Noticing others makes your team stronger.

Pay a favor forward. Everyone knows the good feeling you get when someone helps you out, gives you a ride home, helps with a challenging parent, stocks the supplies without being asked. When someone does something special for you, spread that good feeling by doing something special for someone else on your team.

Remember your manners. You talk about role modeling manners for children, but do you treat others on your team with common courtesy? Say "thank you" when people help you. Smile to show you are happy to see and be with them. If you aren't happy, smile anyway. Being courteous is a conscious, professional choice, not an emotion.

Start helping someone. When you see someone else working hard, join in and give her a hand. You complete jobs more quickly when you are working with others, and it's usually much more fun.

Talk up the team. When you introduce one of your team members to another employee, new employee, parent, child, or someone else, add a few words of praise or information about her. "Let me introduce you to Cindi. She just finished a community service project with the preschoolers that was featured in the newspaper." "Have you met Fong? She works with the toddlers and hikes on the weekends."

Should You Ever Judge Others?

Sometimes judgments are based on an initial meeting of someone, and at other times, people make judgments based on people's actions, performance, or the things they say. Aren't the judgments based on evidence of performance warranted? If you think the safety or care of the children is in any way compromised, yes, you must tell your supervisor and address the issue. You see, that's not judging a person—that's judging a person's behavior. That's all right. Just as there are no bad kids, only children who sometimes make bad choices, the same goes for adults. Accept team members for who they are and encourage and coach them to be the best they can. That's teamwork.

Getting to Know Your Team Members

Here's an exercise you can use in your program to get to know each other better. Ask each member fill out the form below, then add a picture of the team member and hang up these pages in a staff area or use them to create a book. You can also use this exercise at the beginning of a workshop or conference so people get to know each other better. Hang the forms up around the room so everyone can read them and learn more about each other during breaks.

"You Might Not Know This about Me"

1. My name is __________________________________.
2. I've worked here for __________________ years.
3. I was born in _________________________________.
4. Other people would be surprised to know ________________
____.
5. The first thing I do when I get home from work is ___________
____.
6. Some of the people I live with are ____________________
____.
7. One of the favorite things my family really loves doing is _______
____.
8. During my free time, I ____________________________.
9. If I had more free time, I would ______________________.
10. You may not know, but I am really scared of _______________.
11. I'm likely to pull my hair out if _______________________.
12. My proudest moment at work was _____________________
because _____________________________________.
13. To me, it's a fascinating fact that _____________________
____.
14. I think of myself as _____________________________
but others probably remember me as ____________________.
15. If I wasn't working in early childhood education, I would be working as a ______________________________________.

Using the Form as a Team-Building Exercise

Here are some additional instructions for using this form as a team-building exercise.

Supplies You Will Need

- "You Might Not Know This about Me" form for each participant. Supervisors should participate too.
- Current photograph of each participant.
- Something to write with.
- Tape to hang the completed forms.

Instructions for the Exercise

1. Provide participants with forms, their photographs, writing instruments, and tape to attach their photos and hang their completed forms.
2. Count off by two's and partner people.
3. In groups of two (three if you have an odd number), ask participants to complete their own forms and share some of their answers with the group.
4. Take turns having each small group come before the large group. Have one partner introduce the other partner and tell one or two answers, depending on the time you have. Then have the other partner introduce the second person to the large group.
5. After every group has introduced its members, hang the completed forms along with the photographs for everyone to see and read.
6. When you take down the forms, put them in a book and display them in a staff area.

Benefits for Your Team

- Everyone has fun getting to know each other better.
- You usually learn more about one another when you answer specific questions.
- People are usually more comfortable writing than speaking about themselves.

- Hesitant participants are more encouraged when working with a partner or small group than when working alone.
- Introducing another person before a large group is easier than introducing yourself.
- Having a photograph along with the written information helps us to remember the person more easily long after the session is completed.
- Learning your teammates' answers brings your team closer together.
- You remember special things about others on our team.

Idea Stretchers

- Make up your own questions and do the exercise at another staff workshop.
- Have a small group of employees work together to make up questions for another of your program's staff meetings.
- Ask staff a short question about themselves every month. Write the question at the top of a large piece of poster board and ask people to add their answer and name at their leisure.
- Choose an employee of the month or a classroom of the month based on longevity or alphabetical order. Have the employee or teachers in that classroom create a poster or book about each person. Include photographs, information about the person, and fun facts, like favorite food, best vacation, hometown, leisure hobby, high school activities, or special recipe. The list is endless.

35 Ideas to Support Instead of Judge Your Team

1 Offer words of encouragement on a job well done.

2 Help others without being asked.

3 Bring in items for other staff, goodies for the staff lounge, or supplies for art projects.

4 Say "thank you" more often and really mean it.

5 Have fun as a team: go out to dinner, see a movie, or play miniature golf.

6 Ask someone a question about her life outside of work.

7 Be understanding when people are down or not feeling well.

8 Tell another team member, "I like what you did."

9 Give someone a hug.

10 Make or buy lunch for another staff member.

11 Have secret buddies more often than holidays.

12 Put thank-you notes in people's work mailboxes.

13 Prepare program and classroom goals together.

14 Recognize birthdays.

15 Smile.

16 Be nice.

17 Go out of your way.

18 Help staff on the other side of the building.

19 List teachers who have attended workshops, and display the list where everyone can see it.

20 List teacher and other staff who give workshops.

21 Have a positive attitude.

22 Have a message board in a staff area.

23 Say hello to each other.

24 Pair a new employee with a veteran staff member.

25 Empower others with special tasks, such as organizing a book fair or ordering supplies.

26 Recognize other staff for doing special tasks.

27 Keep each other informed of workshops and conferences.

28 Inform others of community events, and local places to eat and shop.

29 Set up a staff workstation.

30 Recognize employment anniversaries.

31 Organize social committees.

32 Solicit parent appreciations.

33 Share parent appreciations.

34 Gather all the items needed for a special project with the children and give them to another class.

35 Let the little things go.

The most amazing thing about a winning team is that although the people who make up that team have common interests and goals, the members are all so different. Different is good, because it brings diverse experiences, perspectives, skills, and ideas. But different can also drive us crazy because it means that others will do things differently. Just as the children you care for and educate are unique, so are the adults with whom you work. Maybe it's time to pull out the baby pictures of those on your team and remember that all of you were once children too. Remember: a winning team starts with you. What can you do to improve your team? It's time to get started now.

OPTIMIZE YOUR KNOWLEDGE

1 What is something about you that you think people use to **judge** you?

____

____

____

____

2 Without using a name, describe a time when you judged someone and discovered that your **assumptions** were incorrect. What were your first impressions, and what was the person really like?

____

____

____

____

3 In this step, refer to the list 35 Ideas to Support Instead of Judge Your Team. Check the ways you have supported others and then circle three ways you will use to **support** some of your team members in the future.

Certificate of Achievement

This certificate is presented to

____

for completing the professional development program:

Winning Ways for Early Childhood Professionals: Becoming a Team Player

__________ In-service hours

Redleaf Press®
www.redleafpress.org
800-423-8309

Gigi Schweikert
www.gigischweikert.com

The author and Redleaf Press have not verified the actual completion of the program by this participant.